THE
JESSE TREE
ANTHOLOGY

Compiled, edited and illustrated by

RACHEL YARWORTH

Dedicated to God, my friend – it's always for you.

And to Mike, Josh, Ben and Daniel –
my most favourite human beings ever!
It's my greatest privilege to love you all.

xxxx

ACKNOWLEDGEMENTS

I want to sincerely thank all the authors who so generously gave of their time and skill to write entries for the book – at times it felt breathtakingly presumptuous of me to edit your work. I am so grateful for your brilliant writing, and for your patience as I got to grips with the scale of what I had taken on. I would gladly work with each and all of you any time. And special thanks must go to Liz Carter not only for being one of those amazing contributors, but also for sharing your many skills in line edit, formatting, and cover design to make this book so much better than I could alone. I am in awe of your talents, and so grateful to God for connecting us.

Thanks must also go to all my behind-the-scenes beta readers who generously gave their time and feedback to help me hone what I wanted to achieve. Joy, Chris, Jess, Fran, Natasha, Alex and Lesley, your contributions were absolutely invaluable – thank you so much.

Huge thanks to Mike and the boys, my mum Jackie and sister Aimee, my Kingdom-writer friends, and my other cheerleaders who have encouraged me, prayed for me, and kept me going when I thought I couldn't do it. You guys are the best.

Finally, thanks to everyone who bought my first book, read it, loved it, left reviews (you have no idea what an encouragement that is!), followed me on social media, and came back for more this time around. You're a big part of the reason I kept writing, so truly: thank you.

May God bless you all enormously!

INTRODUCTION

Since my children were young, my family has enjoyed following the 'Jesse Tree' tradition every year. It's a series of Advent readings that trace Jesus' family tree – a selection of the key ancestors and forerunners who came before his birth that first Christmas.

There are plenty of good Jesse Tree resources out there, and we have been blessed by many of them. But when I looked for one that specifically showed how each story pointed to Jesus, I couldn't find one. I thought it would be great if someone could write one.

At about the same time, I was writing my first book, and I started to meet other Christian writers whose work I love. I began to imagine how wonderful it would be to create an anthology featuring some of their work…

The day those two trains of thought connected, I knew I had to make it happen: there's something about a collection of ancient stories all pointing to Jesus told by modern voices belonging to present-day friends of Jesus that feels really exciting.

So here we are, with lots of stories that are all part of one big story with Jesus at the centre of it all.

I wanted this book to be readable for people of all ages and backgrounds so, for the sake of simplicity, I have quoted the passages from the International Children's Bible (please see the copyright page).

Each passage has been kept short, for the benefit of people who only have a few minutes to spare every morning. For those who would like to read further, I have included Bible references in the footnotes, questions to ponder in your own journal or discuss with others, and short prayer suggestions which you can pray as written, or use them as focus points to add your own prayers to. And finally, you will find simple illustrations in each chapter that you can cut out, colour in, and hang on your very own Jesse Tree as you journey with us through Advent. If you don't want to cut pages out of your lovely book – and I fully understand that sentiment – or if you are reading on an e-reader, the illustrations can be downloaded as a PDF file from rachelyarworthwriter.uk, where both black-and-white and full colour versions are available.

It's entirely up to you how you use the book – whether you just read the Bible passages and devotional readings or use every section. But however you use it, everyone who has contributed to the book hopes and prays that it will help you deepen your relationship with Jesus.

May God bless you richly as you read.

Rachel Yarworth

DAY 1

The Family Tree

A branch will grow from a stump of a tree that was cut down.

So a new king will come from the family of Jesse. The Spirit of the Lord will rest upon that king. The Spirit gives him wisdom, understanding, guidance and power. And the Spirit teaches him to know and respect the Lord...

At that time the new king from the family of Jesse will stand as a banner for the people. The nations will come together around him. And the place where he lives will be filled with glory.

Isaiah 11:1-2, 10

THE FAMILY TREE

By Liz Carter

Are you ready for that time of year again? Time to put up your tree so you can make your home beautiful for Christmas. Do you prefer a fragrant real tree or a sparkly tinsel one? Either way, it's a joy to decorate them, to light up the darkness of winter and bring hope into our lives.

This passage is about a hope-tree that is also a family tree. A tree had been cut down – the Israelites had been battered, exiled, hated. For a while, it felt like the darkness had taken over. But then Isaiah gave them this exciting message: there was going to be new growth – a new king. And this king would be full of the Spirit, just like their rulers of old. Not only that, but this king would be from the family of their greatest king, David, son of Jesse. Who would he be? Would he rescue them from their despair?

It was only hundreds of years later that this hope would be realised in Jesus Christ. Jesus was the fulfilment of these words, with the Spirit resting upon him. And he would become a new hope for all nations, too – a hope that still carries us forward today, even when darkness falls all around.

So when you decorate your tree this year, think about hope. Think about how Jesus came and lived among us and how we still have his Spirit within us, assuring us, comforting us, and empowering us in a world that can hurt. Think about how your future is hope-filled, because though Israel's family tree seemed cut down, Jesus came as a new branch, and so through him you are a part of God's great family tree, along with countless others through the ages. As you prepare for the coming season, then, may you know the peace and love of Christ close around you and within you.

Liz Carter is the author of several books including *Valuable: Why Your Worth is not Defined by how Useful You Feel*. Her website is greatadventure.carterclan.me.uk

DAY 1

Think About It

★ Have you ever looked into your own family tree? Do you know what sort of people are in it?

★ How does it feel to know that, from the beginning, God planned for you to be in his family tree?

★ What does it mean for you to have hope today?

★ How can you share that hope with others?

DAY 1

Pray About It

Dear God,

You are the best Father ever!
Thank you for adopting me into your family.
Help me never forget I'm your child,
Thank you for the hope that you
gave us through Jesus.
I'm sorry for when I let worries take over.
Help me always remember your hope
and share it with everyone.

Amen.

Jesus was the new branch that connects us all
to God's family tree.

DAY 2

Created By Love, For Love

In the beginning God created the sky and the earth. The earth was empty and had no form. Darkness covered the ocean, and God's Spirit was moving over the water.

Then God said, "Let there be light!" And there was light. God saw that the light was good. So he divided the light from the darkness. God named the light "day" and the darkness "night". Evening passed, and morning came. This was the first day...

Then the Lord God took dust from the ground and formed man from it. The Lord breathed the breath of life into the man's nose. And the man became a living person...

The man gave names to all the tame animals, to the birds in the sky and to all the wild animals. But Adam did not find a helper that was right for him. So the Lord God caused the man to sleep very deeply. While the man was asleep, God took one of the ribs from the man's body. Then God closed the man's skin at the place where he took the rib. The Lord God used the rib from the man to make a woman. Then the Lord brought the woman to the man.

Genesis 1:1-5; 2:7, 20-22

CREATED BY LOVE, FOR LOVE

By Maressa Mortimer

In the beginning, God created.

God created the world, He made animals, and He made people. Every evening, God looked at His work of that day and declared it to be good.

On day six, God created Adam. He lovingly shaped him out of the dust of the ground, rather than simply speaking him into being. He was handmade, created in God's image to be like God: creative, knowledgeable, understanding, loving, and made for connecting with others.

But Adam was alone, and that was the only thing that God looked at and said, "It's not good"[1]. So, God made Eve out of Adam's side to be his partner, and that made the world perfect once more. Adam and Eve were made for love: to love and to be loved. Just like we are made for connecting with God and others around us. God had a special relationship with Adam and Eve, walking with them in the Garden of Eden.

The Bible says that Jesus was the one everything was created *by*, and He was the one everything was created *for*. The One who made the world came in love thousands of years later to a world now filled with bitterness, hatred and sadness. He came to rescue people and to show God's perfect love. He gave his life out of love once more to rescue people and to show them perfect love. God created us to love Him and love others, and as we turn to Jesus and accept Him, God's love will fill us again and we will be re-created to love and to be loved. God will once again walk with us through life, like He did with Adam and Eve.

Maressa Mortimer is the author of several books including *The Elabi Chronicles*. Her website is vicarioushome.com

---

[1] Gen 2:18

DAY 2

Think About It

★ What do you think you were created for?

★ Why do you think God created Eve?

★ Who else can you think of who needs to know God loves them?

★ How can you show love today?

DAY 2

Pray About It

Dear God,

You made everything because of love!
Thank you for all the love you have for me.
Help me to always remember you are with me,
even when I feel lonely.
And help me show your love
to all those around me.
I love you.

Amen.

God made the world and everything in it.

DAY 3

The Saddest Day

Now the snake was the most clever of all the wild animals the Lord God had made. One day the snake spoke to the woman. He said, "Did God really say that you must not eat fruit from any tree in the garden?"

The woman answered the snake, "We may eat fruit from the trees in the garden. But God told us, 'You must not eat fruit from the tree that is in the middle of the garden. You must not even touch it, or you will die.'"

But the snake said to the woman, "You will not die. God knows that if you eat the fruit from that tree, you will learn about good and evil. Then you will be like God!"

The woman saw that the tree was beautiful. She saw that its fruit was good to eat and that it would make her wise. So she took some of its fruit and ate it. She also gave some of the fruit to her husband who was with her, and he ate it. Then, it was as if the man's and the woman's eyes were opened. They realized they were naked. So they sewed fig leaves together and made something to cover themselves. Then they heard the Lord God walking in the garden. This was during the cool part of the day. And the man and his wife hid from the Lord God among the trees in the garden. But the Lord God called to the man. The Lord said, "Where are you?"

Genesis 3:1-9

THE SADDEST DAY

By Natasha Woodcraft

It's a funny thing to talk about at Christmastime: The Saddest Day. Christmas is when we're meant to be happy, isn't it?

The trouble is, that suggests conjuring up happiness from inside ourselves is possible. But in truth, the only way to genuine happiness is walking with God in the relationship he created us for.

Adam and Eve didn't understand this. The snake deceived Eve into believing there was more to life than what God offered, using words like, "Did God really say…" to sow seeds of distrust. He made God out to be a liar. He convinced them that knowing about evil was good and choosing their own way was better than following God's way. The result? A broken relationship. Misery. Sin. Something mankind has been trying, and failing, to fix ever since.

God continued walking in the garden, calling out to Adam and Eve, "Where are you?" He knew what had happened, but he wanted them to own up, admit their wrongdoing and start again. Unfortunately, they didn't. They blamed each other and wouldn't take responsibility. So God banished them from his presence.

The next time God came to walk with mankind was when his Son, Jesus, became human. In a different garden, Jesus did the opposite of Adam and Eve. He said to God, "Do what you want, not what I want."[2] He followed God's way perfectly then took the rejection we deserve on himself. He did that so we could walk with God again; so the broken relationship could be fixed.

God is still calling out, "Where are you?" And because of Jesus, we can say, "I'm here. I've messed up, but I want to start again."

Natasha Woodcraft is the author of *The Wanderer Scorned*. Her website is natashawoodcraft.com

---

[2] Matt 26:39

DAY 3

Think About It

★ Why do you think God put forbidden fruit in the garden?

★ How do you feel when you do something wrong?

★ Imagine God is asking you, "Where are you?" What would you answer? Do you believe he loves to be with you?

★ Are you walking with Jesus in your life right now?

DAY 3

Pray About It

Dear God,

Your ways are always best!
I'm sorry for when I do wrong things
and when I try to hide from you.
Help me to remember that even
when I make mistakes, you only want
to help me put them right.
I admit the things I have messed up,
and I don't want to do them anymore.
Please forgive me, keep walking with me,
and help me do what's right.
Thank you for forgiving me.

Amen.

The enemy tempted Adam and Eve to
reject God's best for them.

DAY 4

Saved For A Fresh Start

The Lord saw that the human beings on the earth were very wicked. He also saw that their thoughts were only about evil all the time. The Lord was sorry he had made human beings on the earth. His heart was filled with pain... But Noah pleased the Lord...

So God said to Noah, "People have made the earth full of violence. So I will destroy all people from the earth. Build a boat of cypress wood for yourself. Make rooms in it and cover it inside and outside with tar..."

Genesis 6:5-6, 8, 13-14)

Water flooded the earth for 40 days. As the water rose, it lifted the boat off the ground... All living things that moved on the earth died. This included all the birds, tame animals, wild animals and creatures that swarm on the earth. And all human beings died...

Genesis 7:17, 21

But God remembered Noah and all the wild animals and tame animals with him in the boat. God made a wind blow over the earth. And the water went down... Then God said to Noah and his sons, "Now I am making my agreement with you and your people who will live after you... I make this agreement with you: I will never again destroy all living things by floodwaters. A flood will never again destroy the earth... I am putting my rainbow in the clouds. It is the sign of the agreement between me and the earth."

Genesis 8:1; 9:8-9, 11, 13

SAVED FOR A FRESH START

By Jocelyn-Anne Harvey

What's strange in these verses is that God missed something from the boat-building instructions he gave to Noah. Spotted it? If you've said, "An anchor", you're right. An anchor is essential for most boat journeys across water. So, why didn't Noah need one?

Well, I don't think God forgot. Why? Because of God's attention to detail. Think about it. God told Noah to use "cypress wood" to "make rooms" for animals, from bees to buffaloes, and to "cover it… with tar" so it was watertight. But God knew Noah's family needed to be carried across the floodwater, away from the damage that was happening to the world beneath them. God didn't want them to stay in the same place. He wanted them to make a new beginning.

Without an anchor, God kept them safe through their long flood journey. He cared about each person and animal, knowing that as "the water went down" they were close to the mountaintops that would hug the boat. Then in their new home he painted the sky with colours. A banner of his love and faithfulness. A promise for us today.

What steadies us, though? What protects us when everyday events rock our lives? We all need security. However, we don't need physical anchors to keep us stable. What we need is God's gift of salvation. The ready-made boat that we have through God's son: Jesus. When we believe in Jesus, we have faith, just like Noah's belief in what God said. This takes us away from our sin-filled lives into a faith-filled fresh start.

We trust Jesus will keep us safe. For in Jesus, we have solid hope because we don't rely on ourselves, any other person, or anything else to stop us sinking. As we journey through storms or sunshine, he's holding on and will never forget us.

Jocelyn-Anne Harvey is the author of *Not Knowing, But Still Going.* Connect with her on Instagram @jocelynanneharvey

DAY 4

Think About It

★ The Bible says God was sorry he had made human beings because they were so wicked. Why do you think he saved Noah, his family, and all the animals?

★ How do you feel about fresh starts? Are they exciting or scary?

★ Why do you think God didn't tell Noah to add an anchor to the ark?

★ What do you think Noah's family learned about God while they were all on the ark?

DAY 4

Pray About It

Dear God,

Everything you made is so beautiful!
I'm sorry for the bad things
I do that hurt you.
Thank you for sending Jesus
so I can leave bad things behind
and begin again, any time.
Even when storms come,
help me to be brave,
trusting you to get me to
where you want me to be.
Thank you for fresh starts.

Amen.

God saved Noah and his family for a fresh start.

DAY 5

More Than The Stars

Then the Lord said to Abram, "Leave your country, your relatives and your father's family. Go to the land I will show you. I will make you a great nation, and I will bless you. I will make you famous. And you will be a blessing to others. I will bless those who bless you. I will place a curse on those who harm you. And all the people on earth will be blessed through you."

So Abram left Haran as the Lord had told him. And Lot went with him. At this time Abram was 75 years old...

Then God led Abram outside. God said, "Look at the sky. There are so many stars you cannot count them. And your descendants will be too many to count."

Abram believed the Lord. And the Lord accepted Abram's faith, and that faith made him right with God.

Genesis 12:1-4; 15:5-6

MORE THAN THE STARS

By Rob Seabrook

She woke, sleepy, Dad gently nudging her. "I was dreaming."

"Tell me." He sat down beside her, pushing a strand of hair from her eyes.

She smiled, snug under the duvet. "I was on a beach, under the bright moonlight. Miles of sand. I knelt and scooped some into my hand. The grains were all the same. Beige, tiny, ordinary, formed and moulded by the wind and the waves. I ran my hand again through the sand, and in my palm was a sparkly diamond with shiny light flickering around it. So beautiful compared to the grains of sand. I lifted it high up towards the night sky, and it rose, floating on the air through the clouds. As I looked up, every star woke up and began to shimmer and glisten. Each was like a gemstone. So many different colours, shapes, and sizes. Each one unique, special and precious. So beautiful."

Dad smiled warmly. The day could wait. His love surrounded her as he hugged her. "You know, there are more stars in the sky than there are grains of sand on all the beaches of the world," he said. "A long time ago, God promised Abram that he would have more descendants than there are stars, more than there are grains of sand on a beach. And that all those people who come after him will be blessed through Jesus – like us, a descendant of Abram. Jesus, the beautiful light casting His love over us, which transforms us all, making us like the precious gemstones in your dream."

"Why?" she asked.

He paused. "Because Abram had faith."

She closed her eyes, the pictures springing to life in her mind's eye. Dad's words echoing in her thoughts.

Rob Seabrook is the author of *Beneath the Tamarisk Tree: The Story of a Thief's Redemption*. His website is robseabrook.com

DAY 5

Think About It

★ Abram was old and had no children. How do you think he felt when God promised him more descendants than stars in the sky?

★ How would you feel if God promised you something impossible? Would you believe Him?

★ How did Abram leaving his home show that he had faith in God?

★ How does it feel to be compared to a precious gemstone in God's eyes?

DAY 5

Pray About It

Dear God,

You always keep your promises!
Thank you that Jesus was like Abram,
willing to leave his home in Heaven for our sake.
Help me to always trust you to keep your promises
– even when it seems impossible.
Thank you that even though we are all different,
the love of Jesus makes us all special.
I love belonging to you!

Amen.

God's promise to Abram was incredible!

DAY 6

The Gift Of Joy

The Lord cared for Sarah as he had said. He did for her what he had promised. Sarah became pregnant. And she gave birth to a son for Abraham[3] in his old age. Everything happened at the time God had said it would. Abraham named his son Isaac. Sarah gave birth to this son of Abraham. Abraham circumcised Isaac when he was eight days old as God had commanded. Abraham was 100 years old when his son Isaac was born. And Sarah said, "God has made me laugh. Everyone who hears about this will laugh with me. No one thought that I would be able to have Abraham's child. But I have given Abraham a son while he is old."

Genesis 21:1-7

---

[3] God changed Abram's name to Abraham, meaning "father of many", in Gen 17:5

THE GIFT OF JOY

By Emily Owen

Who is the oldest person you know?

Abraham was 100 years old, and Sarah was 99. They'd wanted a baby for a long time, but it never happened. Now they were too old to have a child. Or were they?

"The Lord cared for Sarah."

He cares about you, too. Did you know that? God cares about every single thing in your life. He cares about your hopes and dreams, things that make you happy, things that make you sad, your worries and your good times. Nothing is too big or too small to share with Him.

He says, "You are precious to me... and I love you... So don't be afraid. I am with you"[4]. You are precious. You are loved. You are safe. God has promised. And if God says something, it's true.

God promised Sarah she'd have a baby. He'd promised Abraham, too. And, after a lot of waiting, it happened. Abraham and Sarah's baby was born.

Isaac. Child of Promise.[5] A miracle. A gift from God. And Sarah laughed with joy.

Isaac was a special baby. He grew up and had children, and they had children, and they had children, until 41 generations later another special baby was born.

Another baby who'd been promised by God. Another baby people waited for. Another miracle. Another baby who brought joy.

Joy to the whole world! A gift from God. Jesus.

He's coming....

Emily Owen is the author of multiple books, including *Still Emily – Seeing Rainbows in the Silence.* Her website is emily-owen.com

---

[4] Isaiah 43:4,5
[5] Galatians 4:28

DAY 6

Think About It

★ When was the last time you laughed? What did you laugh about?

★ Did you know that joy is a gift from God? How is joy different to happiness?

★ Are you looking for joy? Where might you spot joy in your world today?

DAY 6

Pray About It

Dear God,

You are the giver of all joy!
Thank you that you care about me.
I can talk to you about anything and everything.
Thank you for joy and laughter.
Help me to be a joy-spotter,
finding your gifts of joy every day.

Amen.

God's promises always bring us joy.

DAY 7

The Willing Sacrifice

After these things God tested Abraham's faith. God said to him, "Abraham!"

And he answered, "Here I am."

Then God said, "Take your only son, Isaac, the son you love. Go to the land of Moriah. There kill him and offer him as a whole burnt offering. Do this on one of the mountains there. I will tell you which one..."

Abraham took the wood for the sacrifice and gave it to his son to carry. Abraham took the knife and the fire. So Abraham and his son went on together...

But the angel of the Lord called to him from heaven. The angel said, "Abraham! Abraham!"

Abraham answered, "Yes."

The angel said, "Don't kill your son or hurt him in any way. Now I can see that you respect God. I see that you have not kept your son, your only son, from me."

Then Abraham looked up and saw a male sheep. Its horns were caught in a bush. So Abraham went and took the sheep and killed it. He offered it as a whole burnt offering to God. Abraham's son was saved. So Abraham named that place The Lord Gives. *Even today people say, "On the mountain of the Lord it will be given."*

Genesis 22:1-2, 6, 11-14

THE WILLING SACRIFICE

By Claire Musters

God gave Isaac to Abraham and Sarah, but then asked Abraham to sacrifice him. I am sure Abraham was confused, and so was Isaac. He asked his father where the sacrificial lamb was. In verse 8 Abraham answered: "God will give us the lamb for the sacrifice." And, at the last minute, God did.

When I think about why God put Abraham and Isaac through this I focus on the altar. It was as Isaac laid there and Abraham picked up his knife (v9-10) that God stepped in. Why allow it to go so far? Throughout the Bible we read that God wants our whole hearts rather than us distracted by possessions, people, our reputation etc. Even when God lovingly gives us a gift (such as Isaac was) we can allow the gift to become more important to us than God. So here God wanted to be sure he was number one in Abraham's heart.

Also, in Isaac we have a direct link to Jesus' experience. Isaac was asked to carry the wood for the sacrifice, just as Jesus would carry his own cross[6]. Isaac was probably old enough to fight back as his dad started to bind him, so he must have chosen not to. And how did Abraham even get him onto the altar? Isaac must have laid there willingly, which is how Jesus went to the cross[7].

So, this story points to a greater sacrifice. Jesus came to earth to show us the way to the Father, but that meant sacrificing his own life in place of ours[8]. Jesus was even referred to as the ultimate sacrificial lamb: "John said, 'Look, the Lamb of God. He takes away the sins of the world!'"[9].

Claire Musters is the author of multiple books, including *Taking off the Mask*. Her website is clairemusters.com

---

[6] Jn 19:17
[7] Jn 10:17-18
[8] Jn 3:16, Jn 14:6, Mk 9:30-32
[9] Jn 1:29

DAY 7

Think About It

★ What or who do you love the most? Are any of them more important to you than God?

★ How would you feel if God asked you to give them up?

★ How does it feel to know that God loves you so much he gave up his Son so that he could be with you?

★ How can you remember his great love today?

DAY 7

Pray About It

Dear God,

You are the best Father!
Thank you for sending Jesus
because you loved me so much.
And thank you for all the people
you sent for me to love.
I'm sorry for when I make them
more important than you.
Help me to love them but still remember
to love you more.
I want you to always be number one
in my heart.

Amen.

God provided a ram to take Isaac's place.

DAY 8

The Ladder

Jacob dreamed that there was a ladder resting on the earth and reaching up into heaven. And he saw angels of God going up and coming down the ladder. And then Jacob saw the Lord standing above the ladder. The Lord said, "I am the Lord, the God of Abraham, your grandfather. And I am the God of Isaac. I will give you and your descendants the land on which you are now sleeping. Your descendants will be as many as the dust of the earth. They will spread west and east, north and south. All the families of the earth will be blessed through you and your descendants. I am with you, and I will protect you everywhere you go. And I will bring you back to this land. I will not leave you until I have done what I have promised you." Then Jacob woke from his sleep. He said, "Surely the Lord is in this place. But I did not know it."

Genesis 28:12-16

THE LADDER

By Sheelagh Aston

Imagine standing halfway up your stairs. It is a funny place to be. When you look at the top, you see what is ahead. Look down and you see the part of the journey taken. It is when you stand at the bottom or top you see the entire journey completed or to be taken.

In Jacob's case, travelling from Beersheba to Haran to flee from his brother Esau, getting from A to B is his priority. No time for sightseeing or dawdling. Yet it is this encounter on the way to his destination that changes his life and relationship with God.

Also, stairways can be a "bridge" connecting the floors of a building with each other. They enable us to move up and down between floors.

For many people, God can appear a remote "up there at the top of the stairs" figure, especially when things are not going well in our lives. However, the Old Testament is full of stories of first-hand encounters with God: Noah, Abraham, Moses, and Jacob. All of them are drawn into a deeper relationship with God. The gospel tells us how Jesus, via his sacrifice on the cross on our behalf, becomes the bridge, or ladder, creating a way accessible for us to reach God through him.

In Jacob's dream, God's presence in our human lives was represented by the coming and going of the angels along the ladder. Generations later, the angels would bring to Jacob's descendants the good news of God himself dwelling among us in Christ Jesus.

Sheelagh Aston is the author of *Natural Talent*.
Her website is sheelaghaston.com

DAY 8

Think About It

★ Imagine a ladder reaching from earth to Heaven. Do you meet God at the bottom, the top or somewhere along the way?

★ Jacob realised God had been in the place without him knowing. Can you think of a time when you might have forgotten God was with you?

★ How does it feel to know God is always with you even though you can't see him?

DAY 8

Pray About It

Dear God,

You are so good to me!
Thank you for sending your son, Jesus,
to make a way
so I can have a relationship with you.
I want to be with you every day.
Thank you for always being with me,
even though I can't see you.
Help me to remember
I am never alone.

Amen

Jacob's ladder reached all the way from heaven to earth.

DAY 9

Evil Turned To Good

Israel loved Joseph more than his other sons. He made Joseph a special robe with long sleeves. Joseph's brothers saw that their father loved Joseph more than he loved them. So they hated their brother and could not speak to him politely... So when the Midianite traders came by, the brothers... sold him to the Ishmaelites for eight ounces of silver. And the Ishmaelites took him to Egypt...

Genesis 37:3-4, 28

[Later, in prison] Then Joseph said [to the king's officer], "I will explain the dream to you... when you are free, remember me... Tell the king about me so that I can get out of this prison. I was taken by force from the land of the Hebrews. And I have done nothing here to deserve being put in prison..."

Genesis 40:12, 14-15

So the king said to Joseph, "God has shown you all this. There is no one as wise and understanding as you are. I will put you in charge of... all the land of Egypt..."

Genesis 41:39-41

So Joseph said to [his brothers], "Come close to me... I am your brother Joseph. You sold me as a slave to go to Egypt. Now don't be worried. Don't be angry with yourselves because you sold me here. God sent me here ahead of you to save people's lives... This was to make sure you have some descendants left on earth. And it was to keep you alive in an amazing way."

Genesis 45:4-5,7

EVIL TURNED TO GOOD

By Joanna Watson

Joseph was Jacob's favourite son, born to his favourite wife, but favouritism never ends well. As a teenager, his father gave him an ornate robe, which sparked envy, hatred and resentment in his brothers, who plotted to kill him. The oldest, Reuben, pleaded for Joseph's life and convinced them to throw him into a pit instead. Another, Judah, suggested they sell him to some passing traders (more on this tomorrow). As a result, Joseph found himself heading to Egypt. When he was unfairly accused by his Egyptian employer's wife, he ended up in prison, forgotten and abandoned for over a decade.

Upon release, he became Pharaoh's second-in-command and led the nation in preparing for famine. Later, when his brothers travelled to Egypt in search of food, there was a dramatic reconciliation. Joseph forgave them – and God turned what was intended for harm into good.

Like Joseph, Jesus was envied, hated and resented – not by his brothers, but by the religious leaders of his day, who plotted to kill him. Just as Reuben was cowardly, in failing to fully speak up in Joseph's defence, so Jesus' disciple Peter was cowardly, denying he knew him, not just once, but three times. Just as Judah was willing to sell Joseph into slavery, so Jesus' disciple Judas was prepared to betray him in exchange for money. And just like Joseph, Jesus was unfairly accused and abandoned.

But God turned what was intended for harm into good[10].

Just as Joseph forgave his brothers, showed them mercy in their time of need, and rescued them from starvation, so Jesus' death and resurrection enabled God to offer forgiveness, mercy and rescue to all who seek him.

Joanna Watson is a speaker, writer and author of *Light Through the Cracks: How God Breaks in when Life Turns Tough*. Her website is joannawatson.co.uk

---

[10] Gen 50:20

DAY 9

Think About It

★ Have you ever been through a hard time that you felt you did not deserve? How did you come through it?

★ Joseph spent 13 years as a slave or in prison. What do you think he learned through his years of suffering?

★ How do you think it felt for Joseph to suddenly go from being a long-term prisoner to becoming the second most important ruler in the land?

★ How do you think Joseph managed to forgive his brothers after suffering for such a long time?

DAY 9

Pray About It

Dear God,

Everything you do is good,
even when we don't understand it.
Help me to trust you,
even when unpleasant things happen.
Help me to remember that
you always have a good plan.
Thank you that even though Jesus
didn't deserve to suffer, he paid the price
for the wrong I have done.
Thank you that he trusted you
like Joseph did
and has forgiven and set me free.

Amen.

Joseph's robe brought hatred… and then rescue.

DAY 10

The Family Leader

While Joseph was in the well, the brothers sat down to eat. When they looked up, they saw a group of Ishmaelites. They were travelling from Gilead to Egypt... Then Judah said to his brothers, "What will we gain if we kill our brother and hide his death? Let's sell him to these Ishmaelites. Then we will not be guilty of killing our own brother. After all, he is our brother, our own flesh and blood." And the other brothers agreed. So when the Midianite traders came by, the brothers took Joseph out of the well. They sold him to the Ishmaelites for eight ounces of silver. And the Ishmaelites took him to Egypt.

Genesis 37:25-28

... many years later...

Then Judah went to Joseph and said, "Sir, please let me speak plainly to you. Please don't be angry with me. I know that you are as powerful as the king of Egypt himself... I gave my father a guarantee that the young boy would be safe. I said to my father, 'If I don't bring him back to you, you can blame me all my life.' So now, please allow me to stay here and be your slave. And let the young boy go back home with his brothers."

Genesis 44:18, 32-33

THE FAMILY LEADER

By Sharon Hazel

As we saw yesterday, Joseph's brothers hated him so much they wanted to kill him. But Judah intervened: he took the lead with a better plan. He saw a chance to get rid of Joseph without having to commit murder, and as a way of making some money. Judah didn't really care about his brother, though; he was only thinking about himself.

Years later Joseph, through God's protection, had become a powerful man in Egypt. When there was a famine in the whole region, his brothers came down to Egypt to buy grain. They didn't recognise Joseph, but he knew exactly who they were. He set a complicated trap to see how his brothers would behave. This meant Benjamin, the youngest brother, would have to stay in Egypt as his slave.

Judah, however, had changed, and he was no longer thinking about himself. Instead, he cared more for his father and his brother. He was now willing to give up his freedom and his family life for Benjamin to be set free. This is a shadow of the love that Jesus showed for us. He was willing to give up everything for our freedom, that we might be restored to friendship with God.

Later, just before his death, Jacob blessed his sons and spoke words of leadership over Judah – his fourth son – that normally would go to the eldest. Judah was described as a lion's cub – a symbol of rulership and strength. Jacob prophesied that the right to rule would pass through Judah's family *"until the real king comes"*.[11]

Jesus is that King – the Lion of the tribe of Judah, descended from Judah's family and the restorer of true leadership. He is our Sovereign Lord and the One we can trust to take care of us every day.

Sharon Hazel is the author of *To Bethlehem and Beyond! 31 Daily Readings*. Her website is limitless-horizon.com

---

[11] Gen 49:10

DAY 10

Think About It

★ Have you got family members who really annoy you sometimes?

★ What do you think Judah's motives were in trying to save his younger brother?

★ What could have changed Judah's attitude in between the two passages?

★ Why do you think God chose Judah's tribe to be Israel's leaders?

DAY 10

Pray About It

Dear God,

Thank you for the family and friends
you have given me.
Please forgive me for
when I get angry at them.
Help me to forgive them
when they hurt me too.
Thank you for Jesus giving up his life
so I can be free.
When I lead others, help me
to be humble like Judah.

Amen.

One of Jesus' names is "Lion of Judah".

DAY 11

A Way Where There Is No Way

The Israelites saw the king and his army coming after them. They were very frightened and cried to the Lord for help... But Moses answered, "Don't be afraid! Stand still and see the Lord save you today. You will never see these Egyptians again after today..."

Then the Lord said to Moses, "Why are you crying out to me? Command the people of Israel to start moving. Raise your walking stick and hold it over the sea. The sea will split. Then the people can cross the sea on dry land..."

Moses held his hand over the sea. All that night the Lord drove back the sea with a strong east wind. And so he made the sea become dry ground. The water was split. And the Israelites went through the sea on dry land. A wall of water was on both sides. Then all the king's horses, chariots and chariot drivers followed them into the sea...

Then the Lord told Moses, "Hold your hand over the sea. Then the water will come back over the Egyptians, their chariots and chariot drivers." So Moses raised his hand over the sea. And at dawn the water became deep again. The Egyptians were trying to run from it. But the Lord swept them away into the sea.

Exodus 14:10, 13, 15-16, 21-23, 26-27

A WAY WHERE THERE IS NO WAY

By Liz Manning

There's a dramatic version of this scene in the film *Prince of Egypt*. Escaping from the Egyptian army, Moses strides into the waves and plants his staff in the seabed. Wind forces water into enormous walls either side of a path through the sea. The path isn't easy. It's a seabed, after all. There are rocks to climb around, and giant sea creatures swim alongside. It reminds me of the underwater tunnel in a Sea Life Centre. Have you walked through one of those? I have. It was amazing, but I couldn't help wondering how safe those transparent walls were. I wonder how the Israelites felt?

There's an island off the Cornish coast where I live. Usually, you can only get to it by boat. But once a year, the spring tide can be low enough to walk across the sand. Or wade, to be precise. You need a guide to show the way. And you have to come back before the incoming tide rushes in again. The destination is so worth it. For me, an uninhabited island teeming with wildlife and sea views you can't get from the mainland. For the Israelites: freedom, a land of their own.

Don't we all long for freedom from the shame of never quite reaching the mark? Our mistakes and selfishness wiped away as surely as those Egyptians? Just as God made a way through the Red Sea, so Jesus made a way to bring us home. When He died and rose again, He defeated the power of evil and got rid of the barriers between us and God.

So now it's up to us to wade into the waves. Jesus waits to walk with us and show us the way.

Liz Manning writes a blog at thestufflifeismadeofblog.wordpress.com. Her website is lizmanning.me

DAY 11

Think About It

★ Have you ever had a miracle in your life (when God did something impossible)? What would have happened if he hadn't done anything?

★ Are there any difficult obstacles/problems in your life? How do they make you feel?

★ Sometimes miracles come when we take a small step of faith towards our obstacles. How could you do that today?

Pray About It

Dear God,

Nothing is impossible for you!
Thank you that you know the difficult things
in my life right now.
Help me not to be afraid,
but to trust you to make a way through them.
Show me where I can take a small step of faith.
Thank you that you walk with me.

Amen.

God made a miraculous path for Israel
through the Red Sea.

DAY 12

How To Be Perfect

Moses called all the people of Israel together and said: Listen, Israel, to the commands and laws I give you today. Learn them and obey them carefully...

"I am the Lord your God. I brought you out of the land of Egypt where you were slaves. You must not have any other gods except me. You must not make for yourselves any idols. Don't make something that looks like anything in the sky above or on the earth below or in the water below the land...

You must not use the name of the Lord your God thoughtlessly. The Lord will punish anyone who is guilty and misuses his name. Keep the Sabbath as a holy day...

Honour your father and your mother. The Lord your God has commanded you to do this. Then you will live a long time. And things will go well for you in the land. The Lord your God is going to give you this land. You must not murder anyone. You must not be guilty of adultery. You must not steal. You must not tell lies about your neighbour in court... You must not want to take anything that belongs to your neighbour...

[The Lord said] I wish their hearts would always respect me. I wish they would always obey my commands. Then things would go well for them and their children forever!"

Deuteronomy 5:1, 6-8, 11-12, 16-21, 29

HOW TO BE PERFECT

By Matt McChlery

Some months after God dramatically helped the Israelites escape from Egypt, they arrived at a mountain called Mount Sinai. The Israelite people set up camp at the bottom while Moses climbed up to the top. Here, Moses met with God, and God gave him the Ten Commandments that we read in today's Bible passage.

These were the foundation for a whole set of other rules and regulations that the Israelite people were instructed to follow to help them live their lives perfectly. As we read more of the Bible, though, we see that the Israelite people kept getting things wrong. Yet God continued to love and help them.

Just like on the saddest day of all when the first humans decided to disobey God and do things their own way instead, all humans born since then have been incapable of living perfect lives. But God knows that it is impossible to live a perfect life without His help. The law that was given to Moses, which included the Ten Commandments, was to show and remind the Israelites that it was impossible to live a life that was pleasing to God without God being involved.

This is why Jesus came to our world. Jesus was God's son. He was the only person who lived a sinless life – he was perfect. The only way we can be perfect is to give our lives to Jesus and follow him. He will take away our sin, restore our relationship with God and begin to slowly change us to become more like him.

Isn't that perfect?

Matt McChlery is the author of several books including *The Prison Letters: A 40-day Devotional for Lent*. His website is mattmcchlery.com

DAY 12

Think About It

★ What rules can you think of that we obey today? (Maybe at school, work, or the law in this country?)

★ Have you ever broken a rule? How did you feel?

★ Did you know that all God's rules can be summed up into just two? Do you know what they are? (You can find them in Matthew 22:36-39).

★ Why do you think there are so many more rules and laws today than the ten God gave to Moses?

DAY 12

Pray About It

Dear God,

Your ways are always perfect!
Thank you for your rules that keep me safe
and show me the best way to live.
I'm sorry for when I have broken your rules.
I want to be perfect like you,
but it feels impossible.
Thank you for sending Jesus
to be perfect for me.
Please make me more like him.

Amen.

God's rules are to keep us safe and happy.

DAY 13

The Red Rope

Joshua son of Nun secretly sent out two spies from Acacia. Joshua said to them, "Go and look at the land. Look closely at the city of Jericho." So the men went to Jericho. They went to the house of a prostitute and stayed there. This woman's name was Rahab...

So the king of Jericho sent this message to Rahab: "Bring out the men who came to you and entered your house. They have come to spy out our whole land." Now the woman had hidden the two men. She said, "They did come here. But I didn't know where they came from."

Rahab went to the roof and talked to [the spies]. She said, "I know the Lord has given this land to your people. You frighten us very much. Everyone living in this land is terribly afraid of you... So now, make me a promise before the Lord. Promise that you will show kindness to my family just as I showed you kindness. Give me some proof that you will do this. Promise me you will allow my family to live. Save my father, mother, brothers, sisters and all of their families from death..."

The men said to her, "You must do as we say. If not, we cannot be responsible for keeping our promise. You are using a red rope to help us escape. When we return to this land, you must tie it in the window through which you let us down. Bring your father, mother, brothers and all your family into your house. We can keep everyone safe who stays in this house."

Joshua 2:1, 3-4, 8-9, 12-13, 17-19

THE RED ROPE

By Lesley Crawford

Rahab seems like an unlikely example of faith. She was an outsider, not one of God's people. She'd had a difficult life, and hadn't always walked a good way. She was probably looked down on by others. But Rahab had heard of God and what he could do, and she believed. She knew that God was giving the Israelites the land, and she knew that if he was the real God, it made sense to be on his side, so she took action and made a deal with the spies. It was a wise decision!

Because of Rahab's faith, she was saved when Jericho was conquered. She was rescued not because she did good deeds, but because of her trust in God. And, even better, the Bible tells us that she later became part of Jesus' family tree[12].

Maybe each of us is also an unlikely example of faith. All of us have done wrong, and many of us know what it is like to be an outsider, but Rahab's story shows that God welcomes all who have faith in him, no matter who they are.

The symbol of Rahab's faith was a red rope tied in her window – a sign of the promise between her and the spies. It's also a reminder to us of where we are called to place our faith – in God's promise of forgiveness through Jesus' death on the cross. The red ribbons of blood flowing down from the nail wounds in his hands remind us that by putting our trust in him, we can be saved. Not because we deserve it, but because of his grace.

When we place our trust in him, our sins are forgiven and, like Rahab, each of us is also welcomed into God's family.[13]

Lesley Crawford is a regular contributor at gracefullytruthful.com. Her website is lifeinthespaciousplace.wordpress.com.

---

[12] Matthew 1:5
[13] John 1:12

DAY 13

Think About It

★ What does it feel like to be an outsider who doesn't belong?

★ Have you ever felt like you've done too many bad things for God to still love you? How do you know this is not true?

★ Why do you think God wanted someone like Rahab in his family tree?

DAY 13

Pray About It

Dear God,

Your love is amazing!
Thank you for showing that
you love all the outsiders.
Even when I don't like myself sometimes,
you still love me.
Thank you that because of Jesus,
there is a place for me in your family.
Help me to love all the outsiders
the way you do.

Amen.

The red rope was a sign of the promise
to keep Rahab's family safe.

DAY 14

Kindness Reaps Kindness

While Naomi was in Moab, she heard that the Lord had taken care of his people. He had given food to them in Judah. So Naomi got ready to leave Moab and go back home. The wives of Naomi's sons also got ready to go with her. So they left the place where they had lived. And they started back on the way to the land of Judah. But Naomi said to her two daughters-in-law, "Go back home. Each of you go to your own mother's house. You have been very kind to me and to my sons who are now dead. I hope the Lord will also be kind to you in the same way. I hope the Lord will give you another home and a new husband." Then Naomi kissed the women. And they began to cry out loud... But Ruth said, "Don't ask me to leave you! Don't beg me not to follow you! Every place you go, I will go. Every place you live, I will live. Your people will be my people. Your God will be my God."

Ruth 1: 6-9, 16

... later in Bethlehem...

Then Ruth bowed low with her face to the ground. She said to Boaz, "I am a stranger. Why have you been so kind to notice me?" Boaz answered her, "I know about all the help you have given to Naomi, your mother-in-law. You helped her even after your husband died. You left your father and mother and your own country. You came to this nation where you did not know anyone. The Lord will reward you for all you have done. You will be paid in full by the Lord, the God of Israel."

Ruth 2:10-12

KINDNESS REAPS KINDNESS

By Alex Banwell

During the build-up to Christmas, we carefully choose gifts for family and friends, while thinking about those in need and offering gestures of kindness.

Naomi's husband and sons were dead, so there were no men to provide for her needs, but her daughter-in-law Ruth showed kindness in caring for Naomi when she left behind the familiar and safe to go with her to an unknown land. In the fields, she worked hard for long hours, humbly and patiently picking up the grain the harvesters left behind. Her actions proved she wasn't just committing to Naomi, but also to Naomi's God.

Ruth's loyalty was rewarded when she worked in the field owned by a close relative, Boaz, who could buy back Naomi's land. Then it was Ruth's turn to receive unexpected blessings when Boaz married her, sealing her place in the family tree of Jesus.

Boaz rescued Ruth and showed her great kindness, saving her from a life of loneliness and poverty. This reminds us of Jesus on the cross. He died to save us from sin and separation from our heavenly Father: the ultimate act of kindness from a loving God.

Although we see many examples of kindness in this story, it is the love of God that shines brightest of all. He gave Ruth the desire to care for Naomi, and when Boaz found out, God touched his heart to help Ruth. In Romans 2:4 Paul says that God is kind to us so that we will change our hearts and lives... because he loves us! So let's use kindness as a way of introducing others to the love of Jesus, while praying that they will also allow him to reap a harvest in their lives as the good news spreads.

Alex Banwell is the author of *Just Benny.*
Her website is worshipunlimitedministries.org

DAY 14

Think About It

★ Why do you think it is important to be kind?

★ Have you ever practised "random acts of kindness", doing something kind and unexpected for a stranger or loved one? How did it make you feel?

★ How has God showed you kindness lately?

★ How can you show kindness to someone today?

DAY 14

Pray About It

Dear God,

You are always so kind!
Thank you for all your loving kindness to me.
I'm sorry for when I don't notice it
or take it for granted.
Help me always to notice your kindness
and be grateful for it.
And help me to show other people
your loving kindness too.
Let there be a good harvest
in their lives as a result.

Amen.

Ruth sowed seeds of kindness to Naomi
and received abundant kindness from Boaz.

DAY 15

The Shepherd King

When they arrived, Samuel saw Eliab. Samuel thought, "Surely the Lord has appointed this person standing here before him." But the Lord said to Samuel, "Don't look at how handsome Eliab is. Don't look at how tall he is. I have not chosen him. God does not see the same way people see. People look at the outside of a person, but the Lord looks at the heart..."

Jesse had seven of his sons pass by Samuel. But Samuel said to him, "The Lord has not chosen any of these." Then he asked Jesse, "Are these all the sons you have?" Jesse answered, "I still have the youngest son. He is out taking care of the sheep." Samuel said, "Send for him. We will not sit down to eat until he arrives." So Jesse sent and had his youngest son brought in. He was a fine boy, tanned and handsome. The Lord said to Samuel, "Go! Appoint him. He is the one."

1 Samuel 16:6-7, 10-12

God made David their king. This is what God said about him: "I have found David son of Jesse. He is the kind of man I want. He will do all that I want him to do."

Acts 13:22

THE SHEPHERD KING

By Olusola Sophia Anyanwu

God sent the prophet Samuel to Jesse's family to anoint a king for Israel from amongst his eight sons, but Jesse only presented seven! God would surely choose one of them, he thought – after all, they were tall and handsome, and more importantly were brave warriors in the king's army, unlike his eighth son, David, who was a mere shepherd.

Samuel picked the firstborn, Eliab, and, like Jesse, was disappointed when God said 'no' to Eliab and his six brothers. God told Samuel not to get carried away by outward appearances (looks, strength, status, talents, wealth, skills, etc).

David was a shepherd. He had a caring heart, caring for the sheep and risking his life to protect them. He had a shepherd's heart, like Lord Jesus our Shepherd who gave His life for us, His sheep. David, like Jesus, was underestimated and not valued by his family – yet he became king of Israel, just as Jesus became the King of the Jews and *our* King!

Later, David, with no military training, would face Israel's worst enemy – Goliath, a giant! David, trusting God, put his life in danger for Israel and killed Goliath.[14] As a shepherd, he had learned to trust God when fighting off lions and bears who were attacking his sheep, which prepared him for defeating Goliath. Similarly, Lord Jesus defeated the world's greatest enemy, Satan, the devil, when He arose from the dead three days after being killed. His victory over death gives believers eternal life.[15]

Olusola Sophia Anyanwu is the author of multiple books including *The New Creatures*. Her website is olusolasophiaanyanwuauthor.com

---

[14] 1 Samuel 17: 34 – 52 ICB
[15] John 3:16

DAY 15

Think About It

★ Have you ever judged someone by their appearance? Decided you did or didn't like them just because of what you saw?

★ When you look into the mirror, what do you see? How do your looks make you feel about yourself?

★ Only God really sees past our looks and straight into our heart. What do you think he sees when he looks at you?

★ If you are born again[16], God sees Jesus when he looks at you. How does that change how you see yourself?

---

[16] Jn 3:3; Rom 10:9

DAY 15

Pray About It

Dear God,

You see everything!
Thank you that you don't care about whether
someone looks good or important.
You love to welcome weak and broken people
into your family too,
to show your power through all of us.
You only look at our hearts.
Help me to have a heart
that you are pleased with, like David's.
Help me to have a heart like Jesus.

Amen.

David was a shepherd and a king like Jesus,
our King and Good Shepherd.

DAY 16

Light In The Darkness

Now those people live in darkness. But they will see a great light. They live in a place that is very dark. But a light will shine on them...

A child will be born to us. God will give a son to us. He will be responsible for leading the people. His name will be Wonderful Counsellor, Powerful God, Father Who Lives Forever, Prince of Peace.

Power and peace will be in his kingdom. It will continue to grow. He will rule as king on David's throne and over David's kingdom.

He will make it strong, by ruling with goodness and fair judgment. He will rule it forever and ever. The Lord of heaven's armies will do this because of his strong love for his people.

Isaiah 9:2, 6-7

LIGHT IN THE DARKNESS

By Joy Margetts

Isaiah was a prophet who lived hundreds of years before Jesus was born. A prophet is someone who is called to speak what God tells them to speak. Most of the things that Isaiah spoke were to God's people of the time, warning them to stop doing evil and to turn back to a God who loved them and wanted to help and protect them. But among Isaiah's sad messages to the people there were some other messages of hope that God gave him to speak about what God was going to do to put things right in the future. For everyone.

We all know the difference between light and dark. When night comes, we switch on the light so we can see what we are doing! In the Bible darkness is used to represent more than what happens at night. Darkness can also mean evil, fear, hopelessness, anxiety, despair, sin, lack of wisdom, even death. Now if you were living in that kind of darkness, you would be longing for light to come. Light in the Bible signifies goodness, holiness, hope, joy, peace, vision, understanding, glory and life. We know that Isaiah was looking forward to One who was coming who would call Himself the Light of the World[17], the Light that would give life.

The Light to come would be born a child, but also be God's own Son, Jesus. He would come to rule wisely and fairly, to offer comfort and wisdom, to bring peace, and to show us the Father's love. The Kingdom that Jesus would bring would be an eternal Kingdom of hope, goodness, peace and strength. The promise God gave through Isaiah was that when Jesus came, He would turn darkness into light, and death into life forever, for all who would become a part of His wonderful Kingdom – including us!

Joy Margetts is the author of several works of Christian historical fiction, including *The Healing*. Her website is joymargetts.com

---

[17] John 8:12

DAY 16

Think About It

★ Are you afraid of the dark? Even a little bit?

★ Most of us prefer it when it's daylight and we can see everything around us. Why do you think that is?

★ Can you imagine a place where there is no darkness, no evil to fear, no hatred, death, or sorrow? That's Jesus' Kingdom! What do you think it will be like to live there?

★ How can you spread some of that Kingdom love and light today?

DAY 16

Pray About It

Dear God,

You are always with me!
Thank you that even when it's dark,
I don't have to be afraid.
I want to belong to your Kingdom.
Thank you that you want that too.
Thank you that Jesus made a way
for me to belong.
Help me to be a carrier of
your Kingdom love and light
everywhere I go.

Amen.

Isaiah's prophecy promised that light
would come to all in darkness.

DAY 17

An Acceptable Sacrifice

Elijah answered, "I have not caused trouble in Israel. You and your father's family have caused all this trouble. You have not obeyed the Lord's commands. You have followed the Baals. Now tell all Israel to meet me at Mount Carmel. Also bring the 450 prophets of Baal there. And bring the 400 prophets of Asherah, who eat at Jezebel's table."

So Ahab called all the Israelites and those prophets to Mount Carmel. Elijah stood before the people. He said, "How long will you try to serve both Baal and the Lord? If the Lord is the true God, follow him. But if Baal is the true God, follow him!"

But the people said nothing. Elijah said, "I am the only prophet of the Lord here. But there are 450 prophets of Baal. So bring two bulls. Let the prophets of Baal choose one bull. Let them kill it and cut it into pieces. Then let them put the meat on the wood. But they are not to set fire to it. Then I will do the same with the other bull. And I will put it on the wood. But I will not set fire to it. You prophets of Baal, pray to your god. And I will pray to the Lord. The god who answers the prayer will set fire to his wood. He is the true God." All the people agreed that this was a good idea.

1 Kings 18:18-24

An Acceptable Sacrifice

By Joy Vee

Elijah was a prophet who spoke God's word. But Ahab, the king, served a different god – Baal. Elijah organised this spectacular contest between himself and the prophets of Baal. It was simple enough. Each side was to prepare a sacrifice, and the god who answered with fire would be the God the nation served.

The prophets of Baal went first. They laid their meat on the altar and began calling, chanting, singing, dancing, pleading with their god to answer by sending fire onto the sacrifice. But he didn't. This went on all day, with their prayers becoming more and more frenzied. But there was no answer. No fire came to burn up the sacrifice.

Finally, near evening time, it was Elijah's turn. He carefully remade the altar of the Lord, prepared his sacrifice, and had water poured all over it, so it was soaking wet. Then he simply prayed, asking God to prove Himself to the people. Fire came down from heaven, consuming not just the sacrifice, but the wood, the stones and all the water, proving that the sacrifice was acceptable to God. When all the people saw this, they fell to the ground and cried, "The Lord is God." When the people saw that God had answered, they were finally able to acknowledge Him as God.

This reminds me of a similar incident at Jesus' crucifixion. Matthew 27:50-53 describes Jesus's death. It wasn't an ordinary death and was accompanied by an earthquake and other miracles. God was showing that Jesus was the only sacrifice acceptable to pay for our sins. Verse 54 says the army officer and the soldiers guarding Jesus saw this earthquake and everything else that happened. They were very frightened and said, "He really was the Son of God!"

A different sacrifice, a different time, a different place – but the same conclusion. This is the God we serve.

Joy Vee is the author of multiple books, including *The Letters She Never Sent*. Her website is joyvee.org

DAY 17

Think About It

★ Why did Elijah blame King Ahab for the trouble that was happening in Israel?

★ Why do you think Elijah poured water over his sacrifice in the middle of a drought?

★ Why was Jesus' death an acceptable sacrifice?

★ Even though we don't sacrifice animals anymore, God still asks us to put to death our selfish thoughts and actions, so we can serve him in an acceptable way. How might he be asking you to do that today?

DAY 17

Pray About It

Dear God,

You are the only true God.
Thank you that you do all things well.
Help me not to blame you for things
that are a result of my own bad choices.
Help me to love you with my whole heart
and never compromise.
Please show me the acceptable sacrifices
(thoughts and actions)
that you desire from me.
I only want to worship you for ever.

Amen.

God's fire showed he accepted
Elijah's faith-filled sacrifice.

DAY 18

Back From The Depths

The Lord spoke his word to Jonah son of Amittai: "Get up, go to the great city of Nineveh and preach against it. I see the evil things they do."

But Jonah got up to run away from the Lord. He went to the city of Joppa. There he found a ship that was going to the city of Tarshish. Jonah paid for the trip and went aboard. He wanted to go to Tarshish to run away from the Lord... But the Lord sent a great wind on the sea. This wind made the sea very rough...

Then the men were very afraid. They asked Jonah, "What terrible thing did you do?" They knew Jonah was running away from the Lord because Jonah had told them...

Jonah said to them, "Pick me up, and throw me into the sea. Then it will calm down..."

And the Lord caused a very big fish to swallow Jonah. Jonah was in the stomach of the fish three days and three nights...

Jonah 1:1-4, 10, 12, 17

Then the Lord spoke to the fish. And the fish spit Jonah out of its stomach onto the dry land...

Then the Lord spoke his word to Jonah again. The Lord said, "Get up. Go to the great city Nineveh. Preach against it what I tell you."

So Jonah obeyed the Lord. He got up and went to Nineveh. It was a very large city. It took a person three days just to walk across it.

Jonah 2:10, 3:1-3

BACK FROM THE DEPTHS

By Ruth Leigh

In this story we have three main characters: God, Jonah and the fish who doesn't appear to have a name. God asks Jonah to do a job for him, but he replies, "Err, no thanks, I don't fancy that at all." He buys a ticket and boards a boat bound for Tarshish. That's thousands of miles from his hometown: a long way, especially in the days before planes and instant coffee.

Once Jonah is on the high seas, there's a terrible storm. The sailors realise that their lives are in danger because of their passenger and after some discussion throw him overboard. In the meantime, God has a word with a large fish and for the next three days, Jonah resides in its stomach. It can't have been much fun in there. Just imagine the smell of rotting fish, the feeling of lying on squishy fish stomach and the fear that Jonah must have felt.

Trapped in a dark, frightening place, Jonah does the only thing he can. He fixes his eyes on God and promises that he will obey Him. After three days in the fish's stomach, he is spat out on to dry land. Following quite a detour, he walks into Nineveh to preach God's word.

It strikes me that like Jonah, Jesus spent three days in a dark and frightening place – his tomb[18] – before returning to life in all its fullness. Having obeyed God, Jonah's message saves the people of Nineveh from certain death and destruction, just as Jesus gives each of us the promise of a personal relationship with Him and eternal life.

From dark to light, from death to life, from fear to joy. Jonah's story in the Old Testament connects beautifully with the wonderful good news yet to come.

Ruth Leigh is the author of the *Isabella M Smugge* series. Her website is ruthleighwrites.co.uk

---

[18] Matt 12:40

DAY 18

Think About It

★ Has God ever asked you to do something you didn't really want to do? Why do you think Jonah tried to run away?

★ How do you think Jonah felt when the fish spat him out after so long in its stomach?

★ Why do you think Jesus used the story of Jonah to describe the sign he would give to the world[19]?

---

[19] Lk 11:29

DAY 18

Pray About It

Dear God,

You are so kind to send messengers
to those who are lost without you.
Thank you that Jesus – a bit like Jonah –
came back from the dead
so we can all live with you for ever.
Thank you for the messengers you sent
to tell me about your good news.
I want to be one of your messengers too.
Help me have a brave and willing heart
when you ask me to tell people about you.

Amen.

Jonah was inside the "very big fish"
for three days and nights.

DAY 19

The King's Favour

Then Esther told Hathach to say to Mordecai, "All the royal officers and people of the royal areas know this: No man or woman may go to the king in the inner courtyard without being called. There is only one law about this. Anyone who enters must be put to death. But if the king holds out his gold sceptre, that person may live. And I have not been called to go to the king for 30 days."

And Esther's message was given to Mordecai. Then Mordecai gave orders to say to Esther: "Just because you live in the king's palace, don't think that out of all the Jews you alone will escape. You might keep quiet at this time. Then someone else will help and save the Jews. But you and your father's family will all die. And who knows, you may have been chosen queen for just such a time as this."

Then Esther sent this answer to Mordecai: "Go and get all the Jews in Susa together. For my sake, give up eating. Do not eat or drink for three days, night and day. I and my servant girls will also give up eating. Then I will go to the king, even though it is against the law. And if I die, I die."

Esther 4:10-16

THE KING'S FAVOUR

By Jonathan Bugden

Two things leap out for me from the story of Esther:

Firstly, that just as Jesus came at His appointed time, Esther was the person for her day. Their sense of their God-given identity gave them the courage to complete their life purpose. God planned that Esther would be the right person, in the right place at the right time; nothing accidental or random about the timing. Both Jesus and Esther knew who they were so could fulfil their destiny at the appointed time. The same is true for each of us – God wants us to be who He created us to be in order that we can fulfil the destiny He planned for us. It's true for you!

Secondly, that Esther was a recipient of the "King's favour" as he granted her an audience and listened to her request. How extraordinary that you and I can come to the King of kings without fear of rejection, but with the awareness that God embraces us and brings us into his family, because of Jesus. He will guide us, champion us, and look out for us. There is no condemnation or punishment, just the joy of knowing that He adores us, smiles on us, forgives us, and encourages us. He is a "delighted" father enjoying the love, fun and development of his children. It is from this place that we can discover who we are and God's heart for us, and so engage with our purpose on earth.

Jonathan Bugden is the author of *Uncharted – Navigating the Emerging Era.*

DAY 19

Think About It

★ Esther wasn't always a queen. In childhood she was just an orphan. Do you think that helped or made it harder for her to be brave?

★ Sometimes the rules make it difficult for us to do what we need to do. What would it be like to break a rule for the sake of good?

★ Esther was afraid the king might not want to see her and make a way for her to come into his presence. She knew she was risking her life. How does it feel knowing God is *always* pleased to welcome you into his presence?

DAY 19

Pray About It

Dear God,

You are the King of all kings –
the very best ever King.
Thank you for making a way through Jesus
for me to come into your presence for ever.
Thank you for always being pleased to see me.
Please show me what you have put me here to do.
Then give me courage to do it with your help,
I pray.

Amen.

Esther approached the king in faith,
and he welcomed her.

DAY 20

After The Silence

Zechariah and Elizabeth truly did what God said was good. They did everything the Lord commanded and told people to do. They were without fault in keeping his law. But Zechariah and Elizabeth had no children. Elizabeth could not have a baby; and both of them were very old.

Zechariah was serving as a priest before God for his group. It was his group's time to serve. According to the custom of the priests, he was chosen to go into the Temple of the Lord and burn incense...

Then, on the right side of the incense table, an angel of the Lord came and stood before Zechariah. When he saw the angel, Zechariah was confused and frightened. But the angel said to him, "Zechariah, don't be afraid. Your prayer has been heard by God. Your wife, Elizabeth, will give birth to a son. You will name him John. You will be very happy. Many people will be happy because of his birth. John will be a great man for the Lord. He will never drink wine or beer. Even at the time John is born, he will be filled with the Holy Spirit. He will help many people of Israel return to the Lord their God."

Luke 1:6-9, 11-16

AFTER THE SILENCE

By Jo Acharya

Silence.

For so many long years, God had been quiet. His promise of rescue hung in the air like an unfinished song. Would help ever come? Had God forgotten his people?

Though some were losing hope, Zechariah still trusted God to keep his word. But truth be told, he had grown used to the waiting.

And then suddenly—

A dazzling angel. An impossible message. The priest's faith wavered, and his voice was taken from him. God finally spoke, and Zechariah was silenced.

At first glance, we see this as a punishment. But perhaps it was also a gift. For centuries Christians have valued periods of silence as an important part of a healthy, growing faith. Quiet settles us, calming busy minds and healing troubled ones. From one day to the next it may be a spotlight on uncomfortable emotions, a peaceful pause from the demands of life, or a wide expanse where imagination can run wild. Quiet allows us to hear both our own inner voice and the still small voice of God.

Zechariah used his silence well. Those quiet months gave him space to let the angel's words sink in, wisdom to understand their meaning, and time to get ready for the work God had given him to do. When his voice returned, what had grown in silence burst from his lips in glorious song!

As for God's long silence, it ended not in words spoken, but a baby born. The rescue plan faithfully nurtured over so many long years burst suddenly from our Father's heart into glorious life! His great message of love became for us a tiny wriggling child. God in our language, here to show and not just tell: to taste and touch and embrace the hurting world He so loves.

Jo Acharya is the author of *Refresh: A Wellness Devotional for the Whole Christian Life.* Her website is valleyofsprings.com

DAY 20

Think About It

★ Have you ever had a time when it seemed like God was quiet or had maybe forgotten you? How did it feel?

★ How easy is it to keep hoping, loving, and serving him when it's been a long time since you felt him with you? How can you trust him in the waiting?

★ Why do you think Zechariah's voice was taken from him?

★ What are you hoping for today that you have waited a long time for?

DAY 20

Pray About It

Dear God,

Your timing is always perfect.
Even when I run out of patience and hope,
you never do.
Thank you that I can always trust you
to answer my prayers,
however long it takes.
Help me to keep trusting in you.
My hope is in you – the best place to be.
You never fail me.

Amen.

Zechariah's prayers were answered after a long wait.

DAY 21

Preparing The Way

"Now you, child, will be called a prophet of the Most High God. You will go first before the Lord to prepare the people for his coming. You will make his people know that they will be saved. They will be saved by having their sins forgiven. With the loving mercy of our God, a new day from heaven will shine upon us. God will help those who live in darkness, in the fear of death. He will guide us into the path that goes toward peace."

And so the child grew up and became strong in spirit. John lived away from other people until the time when he came out to preach to Israel.

Luke 1:76-80

PREPARING THE WAY

By Anne Calver

I had a dream once where my mum and I were getting ready to welcome guests to a feast. As I walked into the dining room, I realised that the table and chairs were missing, and in their place were two washing machines spinning with clothes. I started to panic, thinking, "How are we going to feed the people? They are coming soon!" I ran towards the kitchen to check that the food was being prepared, but there were clothes everywhere. Where was Mum? Then I saw her outside, hanging washing on the line. I called out, "Mum, we need to get the food ready!"

I really felt that Jesus used this dream to speak to me about preparation for a release of the power of the Holy Spirit and ultimately the return of Christ…

John the Baptist first prepared the way for Jesus by helping the people confess their sins then baptising (washing) them in the Jordan River,[20] before Jesus came to invite everyone to His wedding feast.

Right now, the Lord is preparing us again. He is inviting us to welcome the Holy Spirit into our lives to cleanse our hearts and minds before Jesus returns to take us home. The Spirit helps us know when we are making a mess and enables us to say sorry for our sin, ask for forgiveness, and turn towards Jesus. The love and power of the Holy Spirit moves through our lives to do mighty works in others too.

There will be a great wedding feast when Jesus returns,[21] and we, Jesus' Bride, need to be ready. With the Holy Spirit's help, we exchange our "dirty clothes" (sin) for "fine white linen" (made clean through Jesus). We are loved, forgiven, chosen, and invited by our King to be with Him forever.

Anne Calver is co-author of *Unleashed: The Acts Church Today*.

---

[20] Matt 3:6
[21] Rev 19:7-9

DAY 21

Think About It

★ Have you ever found yourself late for something because you weren't ready?

★ Why do you think God sent John the Baptist to get Israel ready for Jesus?

★ The Bible tells us Jesus will come back one day to take us home to be with him. What can you do to be ready, like the bridesmaids in Jesus' parable[22]?

---

[22] Matt 25:1-3

DAY 21

Pray About It

Dear God,

Your Kingdom is so exciting!
Thank you for washing me clean
of all my sins.
Thank you that Jesus is coming back,
and all those who love him
will be with him forever!
Help me to be ready.
Help me to help others get ready too.

Amen.

John the Baptist lived in the wilderness,
eating honey and locusts.

DAY 22

A Simple 'Yes'

God sent the angel Gabriel to a virgin who lived in Nazareth, a town in Galilee. She was engaged to marry a man named Joseph from the family of David. Her name was Mary. The angel came to her and said, "Greetings! The Lord has blessed you and is with you."

But Mary was very confused by what the angel said. Mary wondered, "What does this mean?"

The angel said to her, "Don't be afraid, Mary, because God is pleased with you. Listen! You will become pregnant. You will give birth to a son, and you will name him Jesus. He will be great, and people will call him the Son of the Most High. The Lord God will give him the throne of King David, his ancestor. He will rule over the people of Jacob forever. His kingdom will never end."

Mary said to the angel, "How will this happen? I am a virgin!" The angel said to Mary, "The Holy Spirit will come upon you, and the power of the Most High will cover you. The baby will be holy. He will be called the Son of God..."

Mary said, "I am the servant girl of the Lord. Let this happen to me as you say!" Then the angel went away.

Luke 1:26-35, 38

A SIMPLE 'YES'

By Jenny Sanders

What a memorable morning for Mary. It's not every day that an angel turns up with a message from God!

Luke tells us that although Mary was confused, she was willing, available, and obedient. Compare her reaction to Gabriel's message with that of Zechariah earlier in the chapter. The priest was educated but still questioned, struggling to accept his news without more evidence. Mary, the illiterate girl from a backwater in Galilee, quickly moved past her first reaction. She listened, asked just one question – and it wasn't the "why?" question that springs so quickly to our own lips – and said *Yes* to God, with Gabriel's faith-stirring reminder ringing in her ears: "God can do everything" (v47).

The Holy Spirit-inspired, freedom song of praise she sang at Elizabeth's house expressed her faith and delight in accepting the task for which she had been specially chosen.

We sometimes skip too quickly over Mary's part in the Christmas story. We imagine her as a blue-robed figure standing quietly by the manger, but she was so much more. There was something beautifully child-like in her trusting response to God, though it wasn't childish. Mary was full of faith, determination and grit. Despite becoming the topic of local gossip and disgrace, and probably forfeiting the traditional wedding anticipated by every girl of the time, she kept her eyes and her heart fixed on the God of the impossible.

Mary's last recorded words in the Bible were spoken during the wedding at Cana, where Jesus turned water into wine. Her advice to the baffled servants was, *"Do whatever He tells you to do"* (John 2:5).

That's what Mary did. We can choose to do the same. Let's keep saying *Yes* to God. As we keep trusting and keep doing whatever He tells us, we'll discover the joy of following Him for ourselves.

Jenny Sanders is the author of several books, including *Spiritual Feasting*. Her website is dancingthroughchaos.wordpress.com

DAY 22

Think About It

★ How would you feel if a mighty angel suddenly appeared in front of you and started talking to you?

★ Both Zechariah and Mary had questions for Gabriel. Why wasn't Mary silenced for hers?

★ Imagine God told you about a miracle that he was planning in your life – would you react with doubt like Zechariah, or faith like Mary?

★ Sometimes God doesn't tell us all the details of our future. How can you trust him even when you don't know the implications of your "yes"?

DAY 22

Pray About It

Dear God,

You are amazing,
and you can do anything!
Thank you that nothing is impossible for you.
Help me to trust and believe all your promises.
Help me to obey even when
I don't know what will happen next.
I trust you, Lord.

Amen.

Mary's trusting obedience was as pure as a lily.

DAY 23

The Trusted Guardian

Mary was engaged to marry Joseph. But before they married, she learned that she was going to have a baby. She was pregnant by the power of the Holy Spirit. Mary's husband, Joseph, was a good man. He did not want to disgrace her in public, so he planned to divorce her secretly.

While Joseph thought about this, an angel of the Lord came to him in a dream. The angel said, "Joseph, descendant of David, don't be afraid to take Mary as your wife. The baby in her is from the Holy Spirit. She will give birth to a son. You will name the son Jesus. Give him that name because he will save his people from their sins…"

When Joseph woke up, he did what the Lord's angel had told him to do. Joseph married Mary. But he did not have intimate relations with her until she gave birth to the son. And Joseph named the son Jesus.

Matthew 1:18-21, 24-25

THE TRUSTED GUARDIAN

By Fay Rowland

Families come in all shapes and sizes. Some are big. Some are small. Some have several generations, with grandparents and great-grandparents. Some are combined families. Families can change and gain new members, like when people marry or have babies or get adopted. Other times, we lose people from our families, and that is painful.

Joseph's family didn't quite work out how he'd expected. He hadn't even married Mary yet, and he certainly wasn't expecting a baby. What a shock! But Joseph trusted God. "What should I do, God?" he prayed.

And God trusted Joseph. In fact, God trusted Joseph with the biggest job in the entire universe. "I want you to be Dad to Jesus," God replied. "I want you to love him and feed him and help him to walk. Teach him to play ball and to use a hammer, and teach him all about Me. And then, when he's grown up, he will teach you."

Wow! What an amazing job. What a huge responsibility. What a wonderful picture of God's love for us. Even though the baby in Mary's belly was not his son, Joseph adopted Jesus into his family and loved him.

And this is what God does for us through Jesus. After he was born and grew up, Jesus took away all the bad stuff that separates us from God. He made the way clear so that we could be adopted into God's family.

Jesus told his friends that God has a home with many rooms[23]. By dying and coming back to life, Jesus made a place for each of us in God's home. Yes, that's right. There is a room in God's home that has your name on the door! We can be adopted into God's family with Jesus as our big brother. What a wonderful family that is!

Fay Rowland is the author of *40 Days with Labyrinths*.
Her website is fayrowland.co.uk

---

[23] John 14:2

DAY 23

Think About It

★ How do you think Joseph felt when he found out Mary was having a baby?

★ How does his kindness to her show what kind of father he would be?

★ Joseph adopted Jesus, and the Bible tells us that we are adopted by God. How does it feel to have the very best Father welcome you as his own child?

DAY 23

Pray About It

Dear God,

You are my good, good Father.
Thank you for adopting me
as your very own child.
Thank you that you are always kind,
always loving, and always wanting
to bless me with good things.
Thank you that I belong to your family.
Help me always remember your love.
I love you.

Amen.

Joseph was a carpenter and craftsman.

DAY 24

Born To Serve

At that time, Augustus Caesar sent an order to all people in the countries that were under Roman rule. The order said that they must list their names in a register. This was the first registration taken while Quirinius was governor of Syria. And everyone went to their own towns to be registered.

So Joseph left Nazareth, a town in Galilee. He went to the town of Bethlehem in Judea. This town was known as the town of David. Joseph went there because he was from the family of David. Joseph registered with Mary because she was engaged to marry him. (Mary was now pregnant.)

While Joseph and Mary were in Bethlehem, the time came for her to have the baby. She gave birth to her first son. There were no rooms left in the inn. So she wrapped the baby with cloths and laid him in a box where animals are fed.

Luke 2:1-7

BORN TO SERVE

By Rowena Cross

I love how we think that us being in control of our lives somehow produces the best results. Augustus Caesar was just the same. He thought that the census was all his plan – when in fact it was part of God's plan to save His people.

Joseph and Mary were both descendants of King David, so they had to return to the place of their ancestors in Bethlehem. So, in faith, they travelled the 70 miles to fulfil their duty. Excitingly, and somewhat plot-twistingly, we already knew they would need to go there, because hundreds of years earlier God had spoken through Micah, a prophet, telling everyone the actual place that Jesus would be born:

"But you, Bethlehem Ephrathah, are one of the smallest towns in Judah. But from you will come one who will rule Israel for me." [24]

And not just that, but also through Isaiah and many others God told us who Jesus was and why He was coming into the world. (Remember Day 16?)

Even though He was God and King of all, Jesus came to serve and not be served. So, it seems fitting that He should be born in a lowly place instead of a palace. Most of the kings up to that point had served themselves, lived in palaces, turned away from God and generally got it horribly wrong. How beautiful that Jesus, the Son of God, the ultimate King, should come into the world and be placed in an animal's feeding trough. A beautiful prophetic picture, even at birth, of the servanthood He expects of us. And through the prophets faithfully recording God's promises to us, we can trust in the power of Jesus' birth, knowing that He came for us too. He came for you, wonderfully unique you.

Rowena Cross is the author of *Be Bold, stop Faffing About and Crack on for Jesus.* Her website is rowenacross.com

---

[24] Micah 5:2a

DAY 24

Think About It

★ Do you think the census was Caesar's idea or God's? Why?

★ Why do you think God planned for Jesus to be born in a poor little place like Bethlehem?

★ How do you think it felt for Jesus to leave the glory and perfect splendour of Heaven and be born as a helpless human baby to poor earthly parents?

★ How does it feel knowing that he did that for you – so he could show you the way to be with him for ever?

DAY 24

Pray About It

Dear God,

All your plans are perfect!
Thank you for sending your son Jesus to earth,
to show us the way back to you.
Thank you for sending him to serve us
when he deserved to be served.
Help me to be like Jesus.
Help me to love and serve others,
to show them the way back to you.

Amen.

Jesus' first bed was a lowly animal feeding trough.

DAY 25

Joy To The World!

That night, some shepherds were in the fields nearby watching their sheep. An angel of the Lord stood before them. The glory of the Lord was shining around them, and suddenly they became very frightened. The angel said to them, "Don't be afraid, because I am bringing you some good news. It will be a joy to all the people. Today your Savior was born in David's town. He is Christ, the Lord. This is how you will know him: You will find a baby wrapped in cloths and lying in a feeding box."

Then a very large group of angels from heaven joined the first angel. All the angels were praising God, saying: "Give glory to God in heaven, and on earth let there be peace to the people who please God."

Then the angels left the shepherds and went back to heaven. The shepherds said to each other, "Let us go to Bethlehem and see this thing that has happened. We will see this thing the Lord told us about."

So the shepherds went quickly and found Mary and Joseph. And the shepherds saw the baby lying in a feeding box. Then they told what the angels had said about this child. Everyone was amazed when they heard what the shepherds said to them.

Luke 2:8-18

JOY TO THE WORLD!

By Rachel Yarworth

Bethlehem's buildings were full to bursting with all the travellers who had come to visit this little old town, trying to find a space to lay their heads. But up on the wide-open hills where shepherds watched over their sleepy flocks under crisp, starlit skies, all was peaceful. Maybe the shepherds were dozing, taking it in turns to keep watch against possible predators. Maybe they were contentedly chatting in low murmurs around the fire, keeping each other awake. Either way, nothing could have prepared them for what was about to happen.

In an instant the soft darkness around them was replaced with blazing glory and wonder as a mighty angel appeared, filling the air with brightness and trumpeting the sweetest of phrases:

"Joy to the world!"

For God himself had come to live on earth, with his beloved children. He had been born as a baby and would grow up to save everyone who believed in him, so we could live with him for ever and ever. What greater joy could there be than this good news of God's loving blessing for us all?

And it seemed like every angel in Heaven excitedly crowded into the skies above Bethlehem to join in the uncontainable celebration:

"Glory to God!"

As the angels then disappeared, no doubt to continue their heavenly rejoicing elsewhere, the skies must have seemed too quiet and dark for the joy now bursting out of the shepherds. They had to go and find the new baby king; they had to share the good news!

So, they ran into town to see Jesus for themselves and to tell everyone they met. It really is the sort of message that is too good to keep quiet! And now it's our turn to let everyone know…

Joy to the whole world!

Rachel Yarworth is the author of *Friend of God: The Miraculous Life of an Ordinary Person*. Her website is rachelyarworthwriter.uk

DAY 25

Think About It

★ Why do you think God chose to announce Jesus' birth to poor shepherds before anyone else?

★ How do you think the shepherds felt to have their usual routine interrupted by a sky filled with singing angels?

★ Why do you think they told everyone in town, instead of going right back to the isolation of caring for their flocks?

★ Who could you tell about the good news of Jesus today?

DAY 25

Pray About It

Dear God,

Your good news to us is full of joy!
Thank you for the celebrations
all over the world today,
because of the birth of Jesus.
Help me to remember you are the reason
for all the celebrations.
Help me to remember the joy
of your good news.
And help me to share it with others,
so they can rejoice too.

Amen.

The angels and the shepherds were the first
to announce the good news of Jesus' birth!

EPILOGUE

I hope you have enjoyed this book and that this year's Advent and Christmas have been joy-filled and Jesus-filled for you. Whether you read alone or with friends/family, I do hope you have seen how it was God's love for us that caused Him to send Jesus to earth to save us[25]– and I hope you have grown closer to Jesus through it.

If this is the first time you have learned of God's love and Jesus' mission to set us free, and if you would like to enter friendship with God as a result, you can! Simply pray this prayer:

Dear God,
I see how good, kind, and perfect you are.
Thank you for creating me
and thank you for loving me.
And thank you for sending Jesus
as the perfect sacrifice to pay for my sin.
He gave his life for me,
now I want to give you my life in return.
Please forgive me for everything
bad and selfish I have done.
I turn my back on all sin
and everything that is not from you.
Thank you for receiving me as your child.
Please fill me with your Spirit
so I can live the life you have planned for me.
Thank you.

Amen.

---

[25] For God loved the world so much that he gave his only Son. God gave his Son so that whoever believes in him may not be lost, but have eternal life – John 3:16

If you have prayed that prayer for the first time, I would love to hear from you! I'm on Facebook and Instagram as Rachel Yarworth Writer, or you can contact me via my website, rachelyarworthwriter.uk. I'd love to hear from you and to help you find resources to encourage you in your relationship with God.

May God bless you richly, now and for ever…

Printed in Great Britain
by Amazon

30879471R00090